SENSORY SCIENCE FUN!

GROSS

Science Experiments

by Harriet McGregor

Consultant: Heather Stockinger, Educator

BEARPORT
PUBLISHING

Minneapolis, Minnesota

CREATE!

Credits: cover, © Egg Design/Shutterstock; cover, © Grebcha/Shutterstock; 4, © tankist276/Shutterstock; 4, © exopixel/Shutterstock; 4, © Emily Li/Shutterstock; 5, © Ninetechno/Shutterstock; 5, © hobbit/Shutterstock; 6, © Valentin Valkov/Shutterstock; 7, © Mega Pixel/Shutterstock; 9, © Anucha Lerdadipud/Shutterstock; 10, © LunaseeStudios/Shutterstock; 13, © Jaroslav Moravcik/Shutterstock; 16, © David Smart/Shutterstock; 16, © grebcha/Shutterstock; 17, © Jarun Ontakrai/Shutterstock; 19, © Pixfiction/Shutterstock; 19, © domnitsky/Shutterstock; 20, © Pixfiction/Shutterstock; 20, © Tobik/Shutterstock; 22, © Manjurul Haque/Shutterstock; 23, © Khamkhlai Thanet/Shutterstock; 23, © Akkharat Jarusilawong/Shutterstock.

Editor: Sarah Eason
Proofreader: Jennifer Sanderson
Designers: Paul Myerscough and Emma DeBanks
Model and experiment assembly: Emma and Stephen DeBanks
Photography: Julie Smith
Models: Svana Arthur, Joseph Myerscough, and William Myerscough

Library of Congress Cataloging-in-Publication Data

Names: McGregor, Harriet, author.
Title: Gross science experiments / Harriet McGregor.
Description: Create!. | Minneapolis, Minnesota : Bearport Publishing Company, [2021] | Series: Sensory science fun! |
   Includes bibliographical references and index.
Identifiers: LCCN 2020007337 (print) | LCCN 2020007338 (ebook) | ISBN 9781647472009 (library binding) |
   ISBN 9781647472078 (ebook)
Subjects: LCSH: Mucus—Juvenile literature. | Microorganisms—Juvenile literature. | Bacteria—Juvenile literature. |
   Science—Experiments—Juvenile literature. | Science projects—Juvenile literature.
Classification: LCC QR57 .M395 2020 (print) | LCC QR57 (ebook) | DDC 579—dc23
LC record available at https://lccn.loc.gov/2020007337
LC ebook record available at https://lccn.loc.gov/2020007338

For more information, write to Bearport Publishing, 5357 Penn Avenue South, Minneapolis, MN 55419.
Printed in the United States of America.

CONTENTS

Science Is Gross! 4

Experiment 1
Snot Science 6

Experiment 2
Make a Mummy 10

Experiment 3
What's Growing? 14

Experiment 4
School of Rot 18

Real-Life Gross 22

Glossary 23

Index 24

Read More 24

Learn More Online 24

SCIENCE IS GROSS!

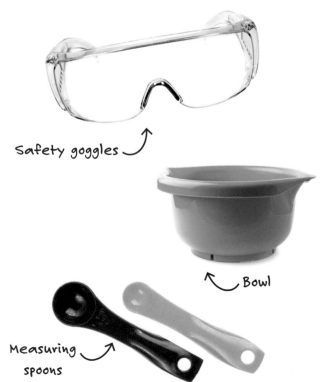

Science is the study of the world around us. It helps us learn about animal and plant life, Earth and space, and energy and motion. Science can be fun, too. It can be gooey, smelly, squishy, moldy, slimy, and—of course—gross. In this book, four fun experiments will introduce you to the wonderful world of gross science!

SAFETY FIRST!

Staying safe is an important part of any science experiment. For some experiments, you will need safety gear to protect your eyes or skin. For others, you will need the help of a grown-up or a friend.

Safety goggles

YOU WILL NEED

At the beginning of each experiment, you'll find a list of necessary materials. Be sure to gather all your supplies before you start. You may already have some of the items at home or school. The others can be found in stores or online.

Bowl

Measuring spoons

Scissors →

STEPS

Each experiment will have a list of steps to guide you. Read them all before you begin. Follow each step carefully.

OBSERVATIONS

Be ready to keep a close eye on your experiment, and record what happens. You can take notes, draw pictures, or use a camera to capture photos or video. Sometimes experiments do not go according to plan—but that's OK! Mistakes can be useful and often help you do better when you try your experiments again.

Magnifying glass ←

CONCLUSION

There is a conclusion at the end of each experiment. This is the last part of any experiment. It will explain how and why your experiment worked.

EXPERIMENT 1: SNOT SCIENCE

You will need

- A liquid measuring cup
- Warm water
- 2 bowls
- Safety goggles
- An adult helper
- Borax

Borax

- Measuring cups
- Measuring spoons
- Gel glue
- Food coloring: 2 drops green and 5 drops yellow
- A spatula
- Rubber gloves
- Dried herbs
- Flour
- 2 plates
- A notepad and pen

Have you ever sneezed and had globs of disgusting snot shoot out from your nose? Follow the steps in this experiment to make your own gross snot mixture. Then, use your creation to discover the purpose of human snot.

STEPS

1 Pour 2 cups of warm water into one of the bowls.

2 Put on your safety goggles. Have an adult help you add 2 tablespoons of borax to the water, and stir the mixture with the spatula until the borax has **dissolved**.

3 Add 2 teaspoons of gel glue into the second bowl. Add 3 teaspoons of water.

GLUE

Yellow and green together will make your snot color!

5 Pour the contents of the second bowl into the first. Put on rubber gloves and mix this with your hands. Be careful—borax can irritate the skin.

4 Add the food coloring to the gel glue and water. Thoroughly stir the mixture with the spatula.

Gross
Science
Tip

You can use white school glue for this experiment if you cannot find gel glue. The gel glue just makes for ultra-slimy snot.

Your snot will look stringy and gloopy in the water.

6 Mix 1 tablespoon of dried herbs with ½ cup of flour. This is your "dust." Put the dust on a plate.

7 Put the snot onto a second plate. Place the snot plate in front of the plate of dust.

8 Stand or sit so that you are just behind the dust plate. Blow hard once across the dust toward the snot. Look at the snot. What happened? Record your results.

Be sure you aren't blowing the dust at anyone. You don't want the dust up their nose!

OBSERVATIONS

Did the dust stick to the snot? How might this be useful when real snot catches dust and dirt in your nose?

CONCLUSION

The snot you made is sticky. When dust is blown over the snot, some dust sticks. This is what happens in the human body, too. The inside of your nose is covered in snot and tiny hairs, called cilia. When you breathe in air through your nose, both the snot and the cilia collect dust. This stops things from entering your body, which helps keep you healthy.

If you use a mirror to look up your nose, you will see a lot of tiny hairs. These are your cilia.

Gross
Science
Fact

Humans can make about one quart (0.9 L) of snot every day!

MAKE A MUMMY

When important people died in ancient Egypt, they were **mummified**. The process of mummification involves some truly gross science. Try mummifying some chicken in this deeply disgusting experiment!

STEPS

The string should rest on the surface—don't pull it tight.

1 Measure around the widest part of the chicken thigh. Ask an adult to help you wrap a piece of string around the thigh. Mark the length on the string where it makes one full loop. Then measure the string from the end to the mark. Throw away the used string. Wash your hands and the measuring tape thoroughly. Record the measurement.

2 In your notebook, describe what the chicken thigh looks like, smells like, and feels like. Wash your hands thoroughly.

Cover the whole surface of the thigh.

3 Use a spatula to mix together 1 tablespoon of baking soda and 1 tablespoon of salt in a bowl.

7 Fill the rest of the container with equal amounts of baking soda and salt until the thigh is covered. Wash your hands thoroughly. Put the lid on the container.

8 Place your experiment in a dry place. Make sure it is away from any pets or young children. Wash your hands again.

4 Put the thigh on a plate with the skin side down, and press the baking soda and salt mixture into the folds of the thigh using the spatula.

5 Fill a reusable plastic container almost to the top with equal amounts of baking soda and salt. Stir the powders so that they are mixed well.

6 Put the thigh, skin side up, into the container, and press it down so it is partly buried.

Gross Science Tip

You can also do this experiment using a fish. At a store that sells fresh fish, ask for the fish's inside parts to be removed. Follow the same directions as with the chicken, treating the inside of the fish body as the skinless side of the chicken.

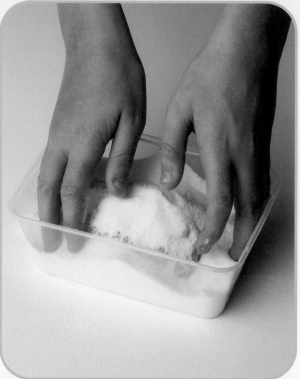

Don't forget to wash your hands after completing step 12!

9 After one week, carefully remove the chicken thigh from the container. Use a paper towel to wipe off any baking soda and salt still left on the thigh. Throw the extra baking soda and salt into the trash.

10 Measure around the widest part of the chicken thigh again. How has it changed? Wash your hands.

11 Look closely at the chicken thigh. In your notebook, describe how it looks, smells, and feels.

12 Repeat steps 5–8 to bury the chicken again. Remember to wash your hands when you are finished.

13 Leave the chicken in a safe place for another week. Then, carefully remove it from the baking soda and salt as in step 9. Measure the thigh again. Wash your hands, and then write down any changes in how the chicken looks, smells, and feels.

OBSERVATIONS

What did the baking soda and salt do to the chicken? Did the color change? How did the flesh look and smell? Did your thigh measurements change after one week? What about after the second week?

CONCLUSION

Baking soda and salt are **desiccants**. This means that they dry things out. Water was removed from the chicken, which makes the thigh become smaller. This drying process happens quickly. You may have noticed a big change in size in the first week and less of a change in the second week.

This is a mummy from ancient Egypt. It is wrapped in strips of fabric. This was the final step of mummification.

Gross Science Fact

Ancient Egyptians removed all of the body's **internal organs** before they dried it. They even used a hook to pull out the brain through the nose!

WHAT'S GROWING?

Experiment 3

You will need

- A permanent marker
- **6 petri dishes** containing **agar**

A petri dish

- A stopwatch or clock
- Water
- Towels
- Soap
- Hand sanitizer

Hand sanitizer

- A camera or notebook and pen

Everyone knows that you should wash your hands before you eat. But why is it so important? Let's find out—and be grossed out—with this fun experiment!

STEPS

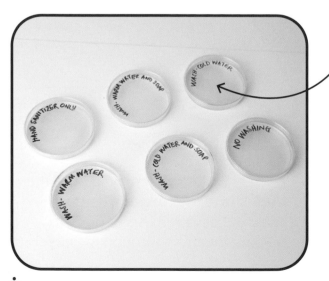

You can buy petri dishes containing agar online.

1 Use the marker to label the lids of the six petri dishes as follows:

- **A.** No washing
- **B.** Wash—cold water
- **C.** Wash—warm water
- **D.** Wash—cold water and soap
- **E.** Wash—warm water and soap
- **F.** Hand sanitizer only

Press your fingers on the agar the same way each time.

NO WASHING

2 Make sure you have not washed your hands for at least two hours. Then, press the fingers of one hand into the agar of petri dish A for 10 seconds. Put the lid on the dish.

3 Next, rinse your hand in cold water (don't use soap in this step). Dry your hand on a clean towel. Press your fingers onto dish B in the same way as you did in step 2, and put the lid on it when you're done.

WASH: COLD WATER

4 Wait two hours. Then, rinse your hand with warm water (without soap) and dry it with a clean towel. Then, press your fingers into dish C.

5 Repeat step 4 for each of the remaining dishes—D, E, and F, following the hand-cleaning notes on each lid. Make sure that you wait at least two hours between each dish.

Gross Science Fact

Germs called **bacteria** can stay alive on your hands for up to three hours. Just one bacterium can **replicate** itself and make more than 2 million new bacteria in just seven hours. Gross! That's a lot of germs!

The more dots you can see on the agar, the dirtier your hands were.

6 Photograph or draw pictures in your notebook of each of your dishes. Be sure to label your drawings.

7 Leave the dishes somewhere safe for about one week.

8 After the week is up, look at the dishes. Photograph or draw them again, and compare them to your first pictures.

OBSERVATIONS

Has anything grown on the agar? If so, count the individual dots in each dish. Each dot is a **colony** of bacteria. Each colony grew from a single tiny bacterium. Do some dishes have more colonies than others?

CONCLUSION

There is almost always bacteria on your fingers. When you pressed your fingers into the agar gel, some bacteria stayed on the gel. Agar gel contains all the **nutrients** that bacteria need to grow. In your experiment, the dishes with the fewest colonies are the ones for which the hand washing was most **effective**.

If you do not wash your hands before eating, bacteria can transfer to your food and enter your body. Some types of bacteria can make you sick.

The lines of bacteria show places where individual colonies have joined together.

Gross
Science
Tip

Wet hands spread 1,000 times more bacteria than dry hands. Try repeating this experiment with wet hands and see how much bacteria grows on the dishes.

SCHOOL OF ROT

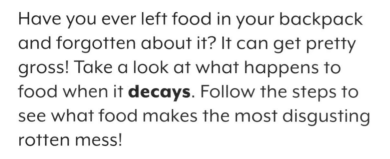

Experiment **4**

You will need

- 6 glass jars with lids
- A banana

A banana

- 1 slice of bread
- 2 lettuce leaves
- A permanent marker
- A camera or drawing pad and pencil
- A notebook and pen
- An adult helper

Have you ever left food in your backpack and forgotten about it? It can get pretty gross! Take a look at what happens to food when it **decays**. Follow the steps to see what food makes the most disgusting rotten mess!

STEPS

1 Line up the six jars. Peel your banana and break it in half. Put each half of the banana into two of the jars.

2 Break the slice of bread in half. Put each half into two other jars.

18

3 Put a lettuce leaf into each of the remaining jars.

4 Put the lids tightly on all six jars. Then, label the jars:

- Banana sunlight
- Banana dark
- Bread sunlight
- Bread dark
- Lettuce sunlight
- Lettuce dark

5 Take a photograph of the jars or draw a picture with labels of each.

6 Which food type do you think will rot fastest? Write your **prediction** in your notebook.

Gross Science Fact

Nobody wants to drink milk that has gone bad. It stinks and tastes **sour**. But did you know that cheese is made from soured milk? Luckily, this is done in a safe way—and the cheese tastes great!

7 Place all of the sunlight jars on a sunny windowsill.

8 Place all of the dark jars inside a cupboard or other dark place.

9 Leave the jars for one week.

10 After one week, look at the jars and photograph or draw them. Do not open the jars! How have the foods changed? Leave the jars in place for another week.

11 Look at the jars again. Draw what you see or take photographs. Write down your observations. Then, ask an adult to help you get rid of the gross food.

OBSERVATIONS

Has your food changed color or shape? Does the food left in sunlight look different from food left in the dark? Were you right in your prediction about which food would rot fastest?

CONCLUSION

Decay is the natural process in which things break down and seem to disappear. Bananas, lettuce leaves, and the wheat in bread all come from living plants. Once picked, the plants becomes less solid. You probably found that the jars left in sunlight decayed faster. Light and warmth speed up the process of decay.

Banana
dark

Banana
Sunlight

Dinner,
anyone?

Lettuce
dark

Lettuce
Sunlight

Bread
dark

Bread
Sunlight

Gross
Science
Tip

Water also speeds up the process
of decay. Repeat the experiment, but
add a few teaspoons of water to each
jar. See how this affects your results.

REAL-LIFE GROSS

We can find gross things all around us. Have you noticed how milk smells and tastes bad if you leave it out of the fridge? There is some interesting science behind all that is gross!

BUZZING WITH BACTERIA

Milk that comes straight from a cow is called raw milk. It may have bacteria in it. Before cow's milk is sold in stores, it is **pasteurized**. During this process, the milk is heated up. This kills any disease-causing bacteria in the milk. But it doesn't kill all the bacteria.

So how does milk go bad? Milk contains a type of sugar called lactose. Over time, the bacteria that remain in the milk feed on the lactose. Then, they change the lactose into lactic acid, which makes the milk lump together. The result is smelly, lumpy, gross milk!

In warm temperatures, the bacteria replicate very quickly. We keep milk in a refrigerator to slow the growth of the bacteria and keep the milk tasting good for a long time. No one wants gross milk!

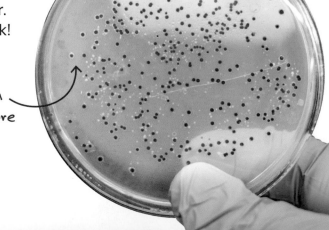

The bacteria in this petri dish were taken from cow's milk before it was pasteurized.

GLOSSARY

agar a gel that contains all of the nutrients bacteria needs to grow

bacteria tiny living things; *bacterium* is the word for one of these living things

colony a group of things such as bacteria living in the same space

decays gradually breaks down

desiccants substances that dry things out

dissolved broken down and become part of a liquid

effective something that works well

germs tiny living things that can cause disease

internal organs things inside the body such as the heart, lungs, and brain

mummified the process of drying and preserving a body so that it will not decay

nutrients things that are found in food and needed by living things to stay healthy

pasteurized heated to make something safe to eat or drink

petri dishes shallow plastic dishes that have a lid

prediction a guess about what will happen in the future

recycled turned into something new

replicate make an exact copy

single-use something that can only be used once and is then thrown away

sour having a sharp taste or smell

The ancient Egyptians even mummified their cats!

INDEX

bacteria 15, 17, 22

decay 18, 20–21

germs 15

make a mummy 10–13

mummification 10, 13

real-life gross 22

safety 4, 6

school of rot 18–21

snot science 6–9

supplies 4

what's growing? 14–17

READ MORE

Martineau, Susan. *Totally Gross Experiments and Activities.* New York: Simon and Schuster (2014).

Masoff, Joy. *Oh, Ick! 114 Science Experiments Guaranteed to Gross You Out!* New York: Workman (2016).

Mould, Steve. *The Bacteria Book.* New York: DK/Penguin Random House (2018).

LEARN MORE ONLINE

1. Go to **www.factsurfer.com**

2. Enter "**Gross Science**" into the search box.

3. Click on the cover of this book to see a list of websites.